A Crash Course in Lesson Planning

How to Create Content for Effective Teaching and Attentive Learning

by Laurie Powell

Table of Contents

Introduction 1

Chapter 1: Factoring in Your Students 7

Chapter 2: Identifying Topics and Lesson Objectives
.... 13

Chapter 3: Selecting the Right Teaching Method 19

Chapter 4: Choosing the Best Learning Material 23

Chapter 5: Incorporating Classroom Activities to Engage Students 27

Chapter 6: A Sample Lesson Plan 33

Conclusion 41

Introduction

I have always believed that teaching is a privilege and a gift. Not all people have the skill to impart knowledge, much less to educate other minds. I am also fairly certain that not every person has the patience to teach. So for a person to go into teaching, he or she will need to have the love for sharing, the passion for enlightening, and the goal of making a difference. Very few teachers ever make a real, lasting impact on their students. The chosen few who do are the natural born educators. They are the ones that have dedicated their lives to enriching minds that are thirsty for information and awareness.

If you are reading this book, then you must be a new teacher. And in time, you will be a good one. This is not to say that new teachers are not already good educators. They can be good, too, but it is a fact that you lack the advantage of being experienced. Nevertheless, all veteran teachers have once been new too. And any old teacher will tell you that *the key to becoming an effective teacher is to have a killer lesson plan*.

Think of a well-prepared lesson plan as your gun in a war. You cannot go into war without your weapon and therefore, you should never go to your classes without effective lesson plans. As you go through years of teaching, you'll become more and more adept at creating good lessons for your classes. But in the meantime, this book will provide everything you need to know about creating effective lesson plans. It also includes a sample lesson plan to help any new teacher get an idea of exactly how to make one. After you finish reading this book, you'll have a solid grasp of what an effective lesson plan is, but more importantly, you will be able to create your own lesson plans for your classes and continue to practice this skill, so that you can become one of those teachers that your students will remember for years to come!

© Copyright 2015 by Miafn LLC - All rights reserved.

This document is geared towards providing reliable information in regards to the topic and issue covered. The publication is sold with the idea that the publisher is not required to render accounting, officially permitted, or otherwise, qualified services. If advice is necessary, legal or professional, a practiced individual in the profession should be ordered.

- From a Declaration of Principles which was accepted and approved equally by a Committee of the American Bar Association and a Committee of Publishers and Associations.

In no way is it legal to reproduce, duplicate, or transmit any part of this document in either electronic means or in printed format. Recording of this publication is strictly prohibited and any storage of this document is not allowed unless with written permission from the publisher. All rights reserved.

The information provided herein is stated to be truthful and consistent, in that any liability, in terms of inattention or otherwise, by any usage or abuse of any policies, processes, or directions contained within is solely and completely the responsibility of the recipient reader. Under no circumstances will any legal responsibility or blame be held against the publisher for any reparation, damages, or monetary loss due to the information herein, either directly or indirectly.

Respective authors own all copyrights not held by the publisher.

The information herein is offered for informational purposes solely, and is universal as so. The presentation of the information is without contract or any type of guarantee assurance.

The trademarks that are used are without any consent, and the publication of the trademark is without permission or backing by the trademark owner. All trademarks and brands within this book are for clarifying purposes only and are the owned by the owners themselves, not affiliated with this document.

Chapter 1: Factoring in Your Students

A good teacher will not just pull out a lesson from her book and use that for all her students. Ideally, teachers should customize the lesson so that it fits specific types of students. So, the very first thing that you need to do before you make your lesson plan is to know your students. Having said that, it is the duty of teachers to know some things about their students so that they can create effective lesson plans that the students can really learn from.

Here are some things that every teacher, whether veteran or new, should always consider when creating lessons for their students.

Age and Level of Learning

Generally, lessons should be prepared and created according to the age of the students. The age of your students will help you determine their level of learning. This is true for all students who have normal learning capacities and are not hindered by any learning disability. In case your students are special children or people with learning disabilities, then other factors need to be considered when making your lessons.

Whether you are teaching elementary, middle school, high school, or college students, you have to make certain that the lessons you create are suitable for your students' age group or level of learning. Always consider whether your subject matter is at the appropriate level, neither too easy, nor too advanced for the learners. If you provide a lesson that is below the level of your students' ability, they will not appreciate it and you will have wasted time (yours and theirs), money, and effort since they will not have benefited from it.

Learning Ability

In many instances, students will exhibit learning capabilities that are advanced for their age. In this case, age should not be the main factor that a teacher should consider when making her lessons. The teacher will now begin to create lessons based on the learning ability of the students. For example, if the teacher handles three senior high school classes, one low-level, one average class, and one advanced, she cannot use the exact same lesson for all these three classes. She can, however, make adjustments to that same lesson so that it can accommodate the needs of the students from all three classes. For example, students who have a different first language may initially need help with vocabulary, and the teacher will need to assist them by breaking down the texts into more manageable portions.

Teachers, therefore, need to be aware of the learning needs of their students. Good teachers have the innate ability to recognize which students need more encouragement and attention and which students need more challenge. When a teacher fails to recognize that a student is a slow learner or advanced for his level, then the student can suffer. The smart student will either lose his motivation to study and the other student can lose confidence. Both can lose interest in school. Teachers, therefore, have a great responsibility in keeping their students motivated and confident to learn. They can do this by preparing lessons that are suited to their students' learning abilities.

Other Factors to Consider—Race, Religion, Cultural Differences

When creating lessons, teachers need to be sensitive about cultural differences, personal beliefs, race, and religion. The classroom should be a neutral place where students can learn. Teachers should never use the classroom to indoctrinate students with their own beliefs, hold debates about religion, criticize other races, or attack people that have different cultural backgrounds. In short, teachers must make lessons that are neutral, and all materials, activities, and methods used for the lesson should be non-offensive to the students.

By being aware of your students' race, religion, beliefs, and cultural background, you can create lessons that all your students can relate to. You avoid alienating students, embarrassing them, or making them feel uncomfortable in your class. By knowing your students and being sensitive to these factors, you can create a positive classroom atmosphere that is conducive to learning.

Chapter 2: Identifying Topics and Lesson Objectives

The Curriculum, Syllabus, and Lesson Plan

The topics for school lessons are unlimited. You can create lessons based on anything and everything under the sun. However, in formal schools, there is a curriculum and a syllabus that every teacher needs to follow. Teachers can't just teach anything that they want to teach. They need to follow the curriculum and the syllabus approved by the school.

Normally, these two are prepared by the department heads such as the Science department head, Mathematics department head, English department head, etc. In some schools, though, the curriculum and the syllabus for a subject are prepared by the department head together with all teachers belonging to that department. In general, teachers are instructed to strictly follow the curriculum and the syllabus. These provide a guideline for topics that they need to teach their students.

The curriculum gives a general outline of what students should learn about for the whole school year and the syllabus contains specific topics and even sub-topics for the subject. The lesson plan, however, provides detailed, daily accounts of how each topic will be taught to the students. A lesson plan is usually created for daily use; therefore, teachers create one lesson plan for every school day. In addition, schools require lesson plans to be made and submitted for approval a week before the lessons will be taught to the class. This ensures that the teachers are fully prepared to conduct their classes and that the daily lessons conform to the school's curriculum and the syllabus.

Making Your Daily Lesson Plan

Once you are familiar with the school's curriculum and syllabus, you can begin formulating your daily lessons. For the lesson plan, schools normally give their teachers freedom to think up the best ways to teach the lesson.

Before you can create your daily lessons, it is important that you know the curriculum and the syllabus inside and out. Remember that schools require teachers to follow the given curriculum as well as the syllabus for any school subject. Many schools sanction teachers that choose to divert from the school's program and will not tolerate lessons that do not conform to curriculum and syllabus. Creating lesson plans take a lot of time and effort and if you produce one that the school will reject, then you have wasted your time and energy. So before you create a lesson plan, make sure that you are working in agreement with the school's requirements.

When you know the curriculum and the syllabus like the back of your hand, it is quite easy to create daily lessons for your classes. This is because you see the big picture. You know that each daily lesson is connected to the next, and you understand the importance of every topic in the syllabus and every daily lesson that you give your students.

Lesson Objective

The curriculum and the syllabus pretty much give you the objectives for your lessons. However, in your lesson plan, you create objectives that are much more detailed, specific to your students' needs, and ones that can actually help them as students and as people. For instance, the topic for Day 5 is Prepositions. In your lesson plan objective, you don't write, "To teach the prepositions." This is an ineffective objective for a daily lesson plan because it is vague and actually too broad.

In the English grammar, there are numerous rules for prepositions, and to teach all of these in a 1-hour lesson would be impossible, if not ineffectual. To understand the proper use of all the prepositions in the English language would take more time than that. Therefore, the teacher needs to choose only a specific set of prepositions to teach in one class. She can either choose the ones that her students need to learn the most or devote more class hours to cover the other prepositions as well. Also, the objective "To teach the prepositions" does not specify who benefits from the lesson, how it helps the students, and there is no clear way of determining if the students learned how to use the prepositions at the end of the lesson.

A good teacher will use the SMART (Specific, Measurable, Assignable, Realistic, and Time-Related) guide for creating objectives when creating lesson objectives for her daily lessons. So to check the lesson objective given in the example above, the teacher can instead write, "By the end of this class, the students would successfully be able to use the prepositions "in", "on", and "at" for telling time and dates in their writing and in their daily conversations." Note that this objective is specific, measurable, assignable, realistic, and time-related.

When the teacher has a SMART objective, she can stay focused on her goal for the lesson. She knows what she needs to accomplish by the end of her class, and she understands what she needs to do in order to achieve the objective. A SMART objective is a clear lesson objective.

In the same way this SMART objective helps the teacher accomplish her lesson successfully, sharing the objectives with the students at the onset of the lesson will give them control and allow them to be more focused in their learning. They will be able to monitor their own success knowing what the lesson entails and what they will have mastered as a result of it.

Chapter 3: Selecting the Right Teaching Method

Now that you know what you'll be teaching and you have a clear objective for your lesson, the next step is to determine the most effective method to impart the lesson to your students. I am sure that you have learned about the various methods of teaching from your undergraduate course as a teacher and have had some practice teaching in your senior year. If so, then you already have some idea about how to teach your class and it helps to keep these fresh in your mind as you begin practicing your profession. By contrast, experienced teachers have formulated their own methodologies, in addition to those they've been taught in school, as they go through years of teaching.

Choosing Teaching Methods

In your lesson plan, you need to indicate the exact way you plan to teach your lesson to your students. A step-by-step procedure of your teaching method is often required in your lesson plan. This will provide a clear guide for you or any substitute teacher that will handle your class just in case. A detailed procedure also shows how the lesson will unfold and how the steps are connected to each other.

To choose a teaching method for your lesson, sometimes, trial and error is needed. For instance, you might think that doing a lecture is the best way to impart a piece of knowledge to your students, however, doing a song or some similar fun activity could be as effective and might even be better received by your students. Don't feel too pressured about choosing the perfect method of teaching for your class. The key is flexibility on the teacher's part. If in your first class the song activity did not work, then try a lecture for you next class. Remember that choosing the teaching method will greatly depend on the students you have. In Chapter 1, I mentioned the importance of learning about your students' ages, learning abilities, and backgrounds. After a lot of trial and error, you will be able to determine the most effective teaching method for a lesson and for a specific class.

Traditional vs. Modern Ways of Teaching

In elementary, high school, and university, a lot of teachers prefer to lecture. And while lectures are effective for university students, it may not be the best method for young children and teens that can barely stay attentive in an hour-long class. Therefore, if you are teaching elementary, middle school, and high school students, you need to have a trunk full of ideas that you can use to keep your students interested and motivated. But don't worry, because as you go through years of teaching, you'll be able to collect a lot of great ideas for teaching your students. Also, it helps that the internet provides an unlimited source of topics, materials, and teaching ideas for teachers today. Back in the days when there was no internet, teachers did manual research and relied on their daily experiences and even the imagination in order to come up with fresh ideas for teaching their classes.

The lecture method may be the oldest teaching method but it does not necessarily mean that it's the best one and it is certainly not the only one. Moreover, teachers should never limit themselves to just one method. There are a myriad of new and more effective methods that a teacher can use to effectively impart her lessons to her students without putting them to sleep or allowing the class to get out of hand due to boredom. Remember, too, that in today's world, using digital technology during the course of a lesson is likely to hold students' attention. To make the most of their natural attention span, you will need to divide the lesson into manageable chunks and ensure that you have adequate activities that resonate well with the various types of learners in your class, whether they are auditory, visual or kinesthetic learners. Know your students so that you can initiate interesting interactive discussions; choose group and individual activities that they can all enjoy and benefit from.

Chapter 4: Choosing the Best Learning Material

Whatever level you're teaching, it is always necessary to prepare materials for your classes. These materials for your lessons can help facilitate better learning for your students. Just imagine trying to explain to your class what a DNA helix looks like versus just showing them a picture or model of it. It helps to prepare learning materials for your students so that they can clearly understand what you want to teach them.

Kinds of Learning Materials

Visual

Visual aids are probably the most common and the easiest to prepare among the teaching materials. Pictures can say a thousand words and a teacher can give her students a clear idea of what she wants to express in just a few seconds. It is effective especially when time is of the essence and when your students respond better to visual learning.

Audio

You may have lessons that require audio. Be sure to provide it. If your lesson is about the different types of birds, you could give your students a chance to listen to the diverse sounds made by various kinds of birds. Or if you're incorporating a song in your lesson, make sure that you prepare the audio devices for your class such as speakers, a music player, etc.

Multi-Media

These days, the things you can do in your class are unlimited. You can watch a movie, a concert, or a play in class. Of course, these should be related to your lessons. All you need is to make sure that you have all the electronic devices for watching these videos. Most schools provide the television, video players, speakers, and everything else for their teachers and students. But in case, these are not provided, you can always bring your own laptop to your classes to help you during your lessons.

Your video clip should immediately spark the students' interest and prompt even the shy ones to form an opinion or have something to say afterwards. Be careful, though, when selecting a video clip for your class. Make sure that it is not too long and that you watch the entire clip beforehand, to be certain that the content is non-offensive and absolutely crucial to your lesson. It will also need to be approved by the school.

Teacher's Materials

In your lesson plan, you have to indicate all the materials that you will need in teaching your lesson. The lesson plan is actually the teacher's main material. Other materials that the teacher will need include the audio, visual, and multi-media materials.

Student's Learning Materials

Teachers will also need to provide the learning materials for their students. These can include student's booklets, answering sheets, materials for activities, etc. When you make your lesson plan, you should also indicate what materials the students will need for every class.

Chapter 5: Incorporating Classroom Activities to Engage Students

Classroom activities are usually frowned upon by many traditional teachers. These old-fashioned educators think that classroom activities are 'playing' and are the exact opposite of learning. This could be why most teachers from the olden times prefer to do a lecture and have the students sit all day and listen to them talk for hours. Fortunately, modern studies on learning have brought light to the role of play in learning. Students from every age, including adult students, can learn from a well-chosen activity.

When choosing activities for your lessons, it is imperative that you select the activities that help your students learn whatever it is that you want to teach them that day. Make an effort to choose activities that are very similar to what they do in real life so that they can see the activity's relevance to their daily life. Also, don't underestimate how effective peer-to-peer learning in groups can be. Teachers should also spend time thinking about the 'M' in SMART (from Chapter 2)—how to measure what the students will demonstrate to show that they indeed were able to learn what was anticipated as the outcome of these activities. With well-planned classroom activities you will have fun teaching and your students will have fun learning and demonstrating that learning.

Kinds of Classroom Activities

There are various types of indoor activities that you can try for your class depending on your topic for the day.

- **Teaser/Warmer/Introductory Activity**

How do you start you classes? Do you just start talking right away about your topic for the day? Most teachers in elementary school always start their classes like this:

"Good morning class."

"Good morning Ma'am."

"Be seated. Our topic for today is about…"

If you're starting your classes that way, you and your students are in for a very boring and ineffective class. Why not start your class with a little fun? For instance, before you start your class, you can use a small activity to introduce your topic. Of course, your students won't know what your topic is yet, but later they will see its connection to your main topic and objectives. The purpose of this introductory activity is to:

- Catch your students' attention and interest.

- Introduce your lesson.

- Make your students' see the topic's relevance to daily life.

Remember, though, that introductory activities should only serve as warmers or teasers for your whole class and these activities should not take more than five minutes of your class. These shouldn't be tiring, so that your students don't feel too exhausted to pay attention to the rest of your lesson. The introductory activity should help you "introduce" the main topic to your class.

For example, if your topic for the day is the Planets, a good warm-up activity would be to pair your students up and have them interview their partner about what planets they know. Give your students two minutes to do this and ask them to report back by pair. This gives them a chance to socialize and at the same time, the teacher can gauge how much her students actually know about the planets.

- **Assessment Activities**

Tests and quizzes help the teacher to check whether the students understood the lesson or not. To help check for comprehension, teachers can give short quizzes to their students in the middle or after the class. It can be a 10-item test to check how much of the lesson the students have absorbed. In your lesson plan, you need to provide a copy of the short test that you will be giving your students.

- **Application Activities**

Many students do not see the connection between their classroom lessons and their daily life. To help bridge the gap between classroom lessons and everyday life, teachers need to provide activities that will help their students see the connection between these two. For example, if the lesson was about the prepositions of time, a good application activity would be to let your students make hotel reservations. This activity will require them to use "in", "on", and "at" as they make their reservations. By doing this activity, the students are given the chance to apply in real life what they have learned in class. When teachers make an effort to make their classroom lessons relatable to daily life, students feel that what they are learning in class is actually useful. Students learn more effectively if they see that the lessons have a practical use. Hence, it is the responsibility of every teacher to present his or her lessons in an effective manner.

Chapter 6: A Sample Lesson Plan

I. Lesson Title: Learning the Prepositions of Time

II. Objective: After this class, the students would successfully be able to use the prepositions "in", "on", and "at" to tell time in their daily conversations.

III. Prepared for: Grade 7 students, Class A and B

IV. Materials: movie clip, media player or laptop, speakers, telephone, sheets of paper, pencil

V. Procedure:

A. Warm-up Activity:

1. The teacher will play a video clip of a person making reservations for a hotel room. The clip is taken from a movie.

Note: The clip should be carefully selected as it should clearly reflect the use of the prepositions, "in", "on", and "at" for telling time.

2. After playing the clip, ask the students these questions:

"According to the clip, where is she going?"

"When is she leaving?"

"What dates did she reserve?

"What time will she be leaving?"

"What time will she be arriving?"

Note: Create questions depending on the movie clip that you have chosen. Just make sure that your students use "in", "on", and "at" in their answers.

3. As the students answer the questions, the teacher writes the answers on the board.

For example:

"In August"

"On Monday"

"In Summer"

"At 3pm"

"At midnight"

"On March 19"

"On April 16, 2008"

B. Lesson Proper

1. The teacher asks the students to look at the answers on the board. Next, she asks them what they notice about these phrases. Students may answer that these phrases pertain to time and dates. Some may answer that they notice the prepositions "in", "on", and "at".

2. The teacher asks the students if they know about the prepositions of time. She will also ask some students if they know how to use them. Are they also familiar with any rules about using "in", "on", and "at" to tell time? The teacher allows the students to explain how they understand the use of these

prepositions. The teacher should encourage her students to speak.

3. After allowing the students to speak their minds, the teacher finally discusses the use of the prepositions "in", "on", and "at" to tell time.

In—used for a specific period of time

Examples: in summer, in winter, in March, in autumn

On—used for an exact date or day

Examples: on Christmas Day, on August 21, on September 11, 2011

At—used for time of the day

Examples: at 22:30, at 6 in the morning, at 10.30 pm, at 3.10 this afternoon

4. The teacher asks the students if they understood the use of these prepositions. The teacher will also

allow the students to ask questions and clarify any points that are not clear. Once the teacher is convinced that all students have understood the lesson, she can move on to the next part of her lesson.

C. Checking for Comprehension/Assessment

1. The teacher gives a short quiz to check whether the students understood the lesson or not.

Here are sample questions for the short quiz:

a. Mandy forgot to set her alarm clock and woke up __ 5 pm.

b. I met him __ the summer of 1969.

c. __ Christmas Day, we usually exchange gifts.

d. I'll meet up with you __ September 19 next year.

e. __ the break of dawn, the mother left her children while they slept.

Note: It is usual to give at least 10 items for your short quiz. These 5 are just examples of possible questions.

2. The teacher and the students provide the answers for the quiz.

3. The teacher checks who among the students got all items correct and which among them failed to understand the lesson. If there are students that need more time and attention, the teacher should take note of them and definitely get back to them later.

D. Application Activity

The teacher explains to her students that they will now do an activity where they can apply the prepositions of time. The activity is making hotel reservations.

1. The teacher asks her students to pair up and create a dialogue about making hotel reservations. They have to use the prepositions of time in their dialogue. The instructions will be very specific as to the length of the dialogue and the time within which the activity needs to be prepared and completed (presented to the class).

2. Next, each pair will use the telephone to call a hotel and make a reservation for two. The teacher takes the students' calls while pretending to be the hotel staff. In doing so, the teacher can make notes on each

student's preposition usage and record any errors in order to provide feedback after the activity.

3. After all students have made their reservations they receive feedback from the teacher.

E. Closing

The teacher provides feedback about the students' calls. She does a recap on the day's lesson and asks her students to remember the proper use of "in", "on", and "at" whenever they tell the time. The students provide the teacher with feedback by filling out exit slips indicating whether they fully understand, or still have something they are unsure of and need further explanation about.

Conclusion

Every lesson plan can provide you with a different experience. Some lesson plans that you make will be successful and others can be a failure. But the key is not to be disheartened. Remember that there is no such thing as a perfect lesson plan. Even the most well-prepared lesson plans can fail. What you can learn, though, is that once a lesson plan does not work the way you think it should or the way you planned it, don't discard it. A good teacher will study why the lesson plan failed and will, make adjustments to it so that it can work the next time. There is also a period of trial and error until a lesson plan can be regarded as perfect. Teachers need to work on their lesson plans every time. The production of a good and effective lesson plan does not stop at its creation. The teacher will need to try it out, use it in her class, observe its flaws, and make notes about what she can improve in it. After doing all of this, a great lesson plan can emerge.

There are some teachers out there who hate the lesson plan and consider it to be mere "paperwork". However, my advice to you as an old teacher is that you should never consider lesson plans as burdensome work. Instead, you need to think of it as a tool, something that will help you in your teaching. A tip to keep you motivated in creating good lesson plans is to always look forward to how the lesson plan will unfold during your classes because the experience is never the same for two classes. It could work for one class but not for the next one. Or it could be fun in one class and more fun in the next. What you should do is to always look out for the factors that make a lesson plan fun, successful, boring, or a failure.

For new teachers out there, the key is to practice, practice, and practice creating lesson plans. Create new ones and always improve your old ones. You can also update old lesson plans so that your students can relate better to it. Don't be afraid to try new ideas and never be satisfied with lesson plans that have worked. Keep in mind that there is always room for improvement so be creative and make every lesson plan a wonderful experience. One thing is for sure, you can always create a good lesson plan if you enjoy doing it!

Finally, I'd like to thank you for purchasing this book! If you found it helpful, I'd greatly appreciate it if you'd take a moment to leave a review on Amazon. Thank you!

Printed in Great Britain
by Amazon